EVERYDAY ST

HOW COMPUTERS WORK

EG ROBINSON

Cavendish
Square

New York

Published in 2019 by Cavendish Square Publishing, LLC
243 5th Avenue, Suite 136, New York, NY 10016

First Edition

Website: cavendishsq.com

This publication represents the opinions and views of the author based on his or her personal experience, knowledge, and research. The information in this book serves as a general guide only. The author and publisher have used their best efforts in preparing this book and disclaim liability rising directly or indirectly from the use and application of this book.

All websites were available and accurate when this book was sent to press.

Library of Congress Cataloging-in-Publication Data

Names: Robinson, Peg, author.
Title: How computers work / Peg Robinson.
Description: New York : Cavendish Square, 2019. | Series: Everyday STEM |
Includes bibliographical references and index.
Identifiers: LCCN 2017054200 (print) | LCCN 2017059297 (ebook) |
ISBN 9781502640048 (ebook) | ISBN 9781502640031 (library bound) |
ISBN 9781502640017 (pbk.) | ISBN 9781502640024 (6 pack)
Subjects: LCSH: Electronic digital computers--History--Juvenile literature. |
Computer input-output equipment--Juvenile literature.
Classification: LCC QA76.52 (ebook) | LCC QA76.52 .R59 2019 (print) | DDC 004--dc23
LC record available at https://lccn.loc.gov/2017054200

Editorial Director: David McNamara
Editor: Meghan Lamb
Copy Editor: Nathan Heidelberger
Associate Art Director: Amy Greenan
Designer: Amy Greenan/Christina Shults
Production Coordinator: Karol Szymczuk
Photo Research: J8 Media

Printed in the United States of America

CONTENTS

1 **Computers** 5

    Women Computer Scientists 12

2 **How Do Computers Work?** 17

    The Foundation of Modern Computing 26

Technology Timeline 28

Glossary 29

Find Out More 30

Index 31

About the Author 32

Computers are part of modern life for kids as well as adults.

CHAPTER 1
COMPUTERS

Computers are part of our everyday lives. We use them for work and for school. We use them to play games and to watch movies. We use them to send messages and emails. We do so many things on our computers without even thinking about them.

What Is a Computer?

But what is a computer? A computer is many things. It is a place to store information. It is a machine that uses electric power. It is a smart machine that learns from special instructions called **code**.

In this book, you will learn how a computer works. Let's start by taking a look inside a computer!

Inside a Computer

Computers are machines powered by electric currents. These electric currents move through paths inside the computer. These paths are made by many electric **circuits**. A circuit is a loop, or

Many kids use computers in school with the help of their teachers.

round path, with doors or gates. When you use lots of them, they can form complicated mazes. The mazes can change, based on information added. The new information makes circuit doors open and shut in the computers. All those opening and shutting doors let electricity

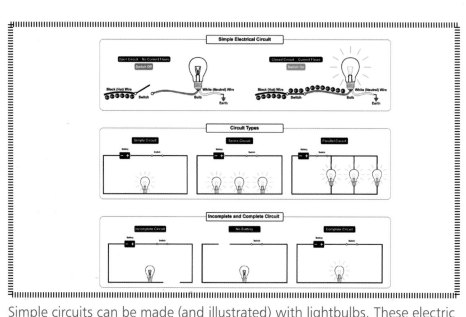

Simple circuits can be made (and illustrated) with lightbulbs. These electric circuits are shaped in loops.

through in complicated patterns. The patterns work together to make a computer.

The image above shows examples of electric circuits. If they are closed, or complete, the circuits carry electricity to lightbulbs. Electricity makes the lightbulbs light up.

Circuits and wires are part of the **hardware** in a computer. Hardware is like the computer's body. It is like the computer's bones, heart, and brain. Computers also use **software**. Software is like the things a computer can do with its body. Software lets a computer solve problems, perform tasks, and think thoughts.

Software is made out of code. Code is a special language of instructions. A computer can do millions of different things with the right instructions.

CODE AND CIRCUITS

How does code work? Let's think about ways you might use codes in your life. For example, have you ever used a secret code with your friends?

Imagine you tell your friend, "If my front door is open, you can come in to play with me. If it is shut, I cannot play today." Your friend can then walk by your door and see if it is open or shut. If

FAST FACT

The very first computer was called the Analytical Engine. It was imagined in 1833 by Charles Babbage, but he never fully built it. The machine was a mechanical computer that used cogs and wheels instead of electricity. Babbage was the first computer hardware designer.

```
110000111111010101010101111
001101001101010101010111001
110001101010100001100011100
101010101010000111001101010
110100111010101100111011011
100110101010110101110101011
```

This string of ones and zeros could be part of a computer program written in code.

the door is open, they know you can play. If the door is closed, they know you cannot.

Your door is like a code, and your friend is like a computer. Your friend will respond based on whether the door is open or closed. The lowest level of coding is called **machine language**. It is the rules for opening and shutting circuits, just like opening and shutting doors.

WOMEN COMPUTER SCIENTISTS

During World War II, many advances were made in science and technology. Both sides knew that having the best tools and weapons could help them win the war.

Grace Hopper helped create the first computer languages.

Men with technical training were assigned to do research jobs rather than fight. But there were far more women than men available for research jobs. It was a special time for women in science. For the first time, women were picked for the best science

teams. These women helped create early computers, including the Colossus in Britain and, later, the ENIAC in the United States.

Grace Hopper joined the US Navy in World War II. She did mathematical research. She was one of the first people who imagined the idea of **advanced programming languages**. She helped develop COBOL, one of the first advanced programming languages. Programmers still use this language today.

Computer codes can be very complicated. To understand how complicated codes can be, imagine a house with thousands of doors. Imagine thousands of open and closed doors that all mean different things.

FAST FACT

Ada Lovelace developed the very first programming language. She was the daughter of the poet Lord Byron. She was a very good mathematician. Charles Babbage asked her to develop the system that would allow his Analytical Engine to perform useful tasks. She was the first computer software designer.

Most programmers do not use machine
language. They use advanced programming
languages. These languages let people use
human words to tell the computer how to
do things.

Programmers create software that tells a
computer's hardware what to do. The hardware
and software work together to complete tasks.
A task can be solving a math problem. A task
can be running a video game.

Hardware designers and software designers
also work together. They help make a computer
do what you want it to do.

This is an early model of an Apple desktop personal computer.
It had fewer options than a modern smartphone.

CHAPTER 2
HOW DO COMPUTERS WORK?

Computers work by sending a thread of electricity (or an electric current) through a maze of circuits. Circuits are like doors that open and shut. The electricity follows the path made by the open doors.

A computer programmer decides how an electric current moves through a circuit. A programmer uses code to make a pattern in the maze. In this pattern, some doors open and some doors shut. The current moves through the open doors of the maze. This way, the programmer teaches the computer to see patterns and make choices.

Early programmers had to imagine a way to use open and shut circuits to represent large numbers. They needed to use computers for complex math. All they had to work with were circuits—open ones and closed ones. Open circuits kept the electric current from passing— there was no connection. Closed circuits completed the path to let the electric current move on. The answer was **binary** code.

Binary Code

In Latin, "bi" means "two." In binary code, there are only two symbols: the number one and the number zero. Binary code is a way of counting by twos.

Binary counts by two numbers—zero and one. Zero and one also mean "off" and "on," or an open circuit versus a closed circuit. A current can either pass through a circuit or it can't. If it can, in binary code it means a one. If it can't, it's a zero.

Have you ever played Reversi? This is a game played with black and white stones. Players add stones to the board. If a set of white stones is caught between two black stones, all the trapped white stones flip, turning black.

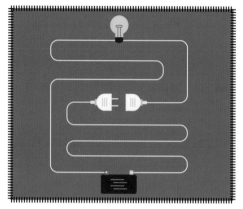

The simplest of circuits includes an on/off or open/shut gate.

Computer codes can change circuits in similar ways. The information the user adds changes things, like new stones added to a Reversi game. Games like Reversi can show how open and shut circuits—black and white— can make complicated patterns that change when you add new information, allowing the computer to do very complicated things.

Binary code can mean more than just "zero" and "one." A series of binary numbers, or a pattern of open and closed circuits, can be used to represent more complicated information. For example, a group of zeros and ones could stand for a very large number, or even a word.

GROUPING CIRCUITS

Computer circuits are grouped in different ways. The basic single circuit is called a **bit** (BInary digiT). It can carry only a little "bit" of information—a single zero or one. A group of eight circuits together is called a byte. For a

FAST FACT

The code system that lets numbers replace letters in computer software is called ASCII, which stands for American Standard Code for Information Interchange.

long time, a byte was the standard grouping for computers. Today, the most common groups are thirty-two bits (four bytes) and sixty-four bits (eight bytes).

These are ways of arranging circuits to let you say more and more complicated things. This is what makes computers so powerful. The more circuits there are in a computer, the more patterns you can use. Each pattern can mean many things, depending on choices you make in your code.

A History of Computers

Modern computers were developed during and after World War II. During that war, both sides made big improvements in science and secret codes. These improvements took large amounts of difficult math. This math needed to be done very fast. Early modern computers were made to help break codes.

After the war was over, scientists continued to explore the things they had learned. In 1946, two engineers named J. Presper Eckert and John Mauchly built the first general computer. It was called ENIAC (Electronic Numerical Integrator and Computer). This new machine could do complicated math more

The Space Race, which occurred after World War II, depended on computers.

quickly than humans could. It helped scientists make new discoveries.

The first computers were huge! ENIAC filled an entire large room, but it could only do a little more than a calculator. Scientists worked to make computers do many different things. They worked to make computers smaller, faster, and smarter.

One of the reasons scientists worked to make computers smaller after the war was that America and Russia were competing against each other. Both sides wanted to get to the moon first. This competition is called the Space Race.

A computer the size of a large room could not fit into a spaceship. The rooms in a spaceship are very small. Smaller computers were needed to steer and control a spaceship.

These computer parts from 1975 were much smaller than those of ENIAC.

Thanks to the hard work of many scientists, today's computers are much smaller and more powerful. The computers in a simple cell phone are 1,800 times more powerful than the ENIAC, and they can fit in the palm of your hand!

FAST FACT

Computers are recycled to get back the precious metals like gold and silver that make the computer's circuits.

During World War II, Alan Turing was one of the most important people decoding German secret messages. He worked at a government base at Bletchley Park, a mansion and estate in England. There, he was part of a team of hundreds of engineers, mathematicians, logicians, and code breakers.

Alan Turing at age sixteen. Turing's ideas shaped the modern study of computer science.

Turing used mathematics and logic to decode German messages. But he was also a brilliant engineer, and he worked with others to develop some of the earliest specialized computers. This work formed part of the foundation of modern computing.

Turing's early computers did nothing but help break enemy codes. After World War II, however, he went on to develop computers for more general work. His writings and his ideas about computing are some of the most important ever produced. Like Grace Hopper, he understood what computers were—and what they could become with the correct design and programming.

Alan Turing died in 1954, at the age of forty-one, but his contributions are celebrated and used to this day.

1833   Charles Babbage starts work on his Analytical Engine.

1843   Ada Lovelace describes how Babbage's Analytical Engine could be programmed to perform calculations.

1939   World War II begins. During the war, Alan Turing and others develop machines for decoding enemy messages.

1946   J. Presper Eckert and John Mauchly develop ENIAC, the first general computer.

1975   The first personal computer, the Altair, is released to the public.

GLOSSARY

advanced programming languages Coding languages that use human words, phrases, and symbols.

binary A system of counting in twos, using ones and zeros.

bit One circuit, or a single one or zero in binary counting.

circuit A loop in the path electricity follows through a computer, with gates or doors that can be open or shut.

code Computer programming grew out of secret codes in World War II. Codes and computer programs are a lot alike, so programming came to be called "coding."

hardware The "body" of a computer, including wires, circuits, and chips.

machine language The lowest forms of computer language, based on binary code.

software The instructions allowing a computer to do tasks.

FIND OUT MORE

BOOKS

Aloian, Sam. *How a Computer Is Made*. Engineering Our World. New York: Gareth Stevens, 2016.

Taylor-Butler, Christine. *Computers*. A True Book. New York: Scholastic, 2016.

WEBSITES

The Problem Site: Binary Code

https://www.theproblemsite.com/reference/
mathematics/codes/binary-code

Scratch Design Studio

https://scratch.mit.edu

INDEX

Page numbers in **boldface** are illustrations.

advanced programming languages, 13, 15

Analytical Engine, 10, 14

ASCII, 21

Babbage, Charles, 10, **10**, 14

binary, **11**, 18–21

bit, 21–22

circuit, 6–9, **8**, 11, 17–22, **20**, 25

code, 6, 9–11, 11, 14, 18–23, 26–27

electric current, 6–8, 8, 17–19, 20

ENIAC, 13, 23–25

hardware, 9–10, 15

Hopper, Grace, **12**, 13, 27

Lovelace, Ada, 14, **14**

machine language, 11, 15

software, 9, 14–15, 21

Space Race, 24–25

Turing, Alan, 26–27, **26**

World War II, 12–13, 22–23, 26–27

ABOUT THE AUTHOR

Peg Robinson is a writer and editor specializing in researched educational materials and white papers. She graduated from the University of California at Santa Barbara in 2008, with honors, and attended Pacifica Graduate Institution. She served for two years as a docent for Opus Archives, focusing on converting historically significant audio recordings to digital format, securing valuable material in a less fragile recording medium. She lives in Rhode Island, with her daughter and her cat and dog.